THE BLUFFER'S GUIDE® TO UNIVERSITY

ROBERT AINSLEY

D1375212

Oval Books

Published by Oval Books
335 Kennington Road
London SE11 4QE
United Kingdom

Telephone: +44 (0)20 7582 7123
Fax: +44 (0)20 7582 1022
E-mail: info@ovalbooks.com
Web site: www.ovalbooks.com

First published by Ravette Publishing, 1988
Reprinted/updated: 1991,1992,1993,1994,1996,
1997,1998

First published by Oval Books, 1999
Revised 2000, reprinted 2001

Series Editor – Anne Tauté

Cover designer – Jim Wire, Quantum
Printer – Cox & Wyman Ltd
Producer – Oval Projects Ltd

The Bluffer's Guides® series is based
on an original idea by Peter Wolfe.

The Bluffer's Guide®, The Bluffer's Guides®,
Bluffer's®, and Bluff Your Way® are
Registered Trademarks.

ISBN: 1-902825-66-7

CONTENTS

INTRODUCTION

The important thing about going to university is the experience. You can throw yourself into a wide range of things wholeheartedly in a way that is virtually impossible when you have a full-time job – things like debt, manic depression, and canals. And there are so many benefits – lots of like minded people to mix with, some of whom may actually become lifelong friends, virtually no responsibility, and a lot of opportunity to enjoy yourself.

A university education used to mean a handful of Latin quotes and a few parroted statements about great philosophers. It had no practical use. It was only a means to an end; a series of key words and right-answers in a handful of narrow and dead subjects of no use to anyone. Nowadays everything is different. The student has literally hundreds of exciting and interesting courses to choose from – everything from Abba Songs to Zulu Studies – in which to learn the series of key words and right-answers of no use to anyone.

There are generally four good reasons given for going to university:

1. It broadens the mind.
2. You make friends from a wide range of backgrounds.
3. Your earning potential is increased.
4. You get things out of university that will stay with you for the rest of your life.

However it is often overlooked that:

1. Being surrounded by people of your own age and studying the same subject broadens your mind almost as much as if you had spent the three years with people in real life.

2. You can also make enemies from a wide range of backgrounds.

3. By becoming a student for three years, you lag so much behind the 16-year-old school leaver of the same ability who is earning three times your starting salary, that it can take you several years to catch up.

4. The sort of things you get out of University that will stay with you all your life are things like overdrafts and herpes.

The bluffer knows that there is only one reason for going to university. You can spend three years wearing whatever you like, travelling for nothing, drinking too much, going to parties, avoiding responsibility and spending borrowed money, and no-one will mind in the least.

In fact, the system is specifically set up to enable you to do this. By giving you no worthwhile job to do and no money to do it with, it prepares you for life in the outside world afterwards. For all its faults – and it would take a doctoral thesis to list them – the university system does perform a range of valuable services to the community. It's just that teaching students isn't one of them.

As in real life, the ones who succeed at university are not the ones with talent, drive, or the right connections. Or even the ability to read and write. It is those who give the appearance of doing so.

The object of the exercise, therefore, should be to bluff your way through three or four years of university with the maximum enjoyment and minimum inconvenience. Then you can honestly say that your university experience has set you up for life.

THE BASICS

Aims of the University

Don't be fooled into thinking that a university is an institution for teaching. Universities are businesses which make money by charging foreign students high tuition fees, and by having conferences of Swedish dentists and American psychologists during the summer vacations. They take you on as a sideline, not because they want to or because there is money in it, but because the conference season is slack during term time.

Universities do a great deal for the academic world, of course – by keeping otherwise unemployable people in jobs. Don't make the mistake of thinking they are interested in your welfare. If you have some sort of meeting with the university authorities at some time, though you put forward valid and eminently sensible notions, such as for the condom dispensers on campus to be free of charge, your proposals will be turned down. They are thrown out by the administrators because they will 'create a precedent', i.e. there is no reason why you can't do the obviously right thing so long as you don't do it for the first time.

Your Aims

At university, unlike school, you are free to decide for yourself when, and if, you will work. This is unlike school, where you have to, and real life, where you won't be able to. You are not there to learn but to earn a degree, whose three purposes are:

1. To reassure your parents that when you spent your vacations inter-railing round Europe with six

friends you were actually doing field work for your dissertation on the American Civil War.

2. To make you eligible for student loans while you are studying, but ineligible for housing benefit or income support, which works out cheaper for them than if you were merely unemployed.

3. To convince potential employers that, despite your application form for the job and your covering letter, you are actually quite clever.

Universities give first, second and third class degrees, and fails, in 'finals', the final examinations. These are much like the rail services of crumbling third-world economies, like Britain. The first class is impressive but can only be gained at great expense and is only normally taken by those who mean business; the second class is economical, perfectly respectable and suits all practical purposes. The third is equivalent to the guards van; extremely uncomfortable and full of those who couldn't fit in.

Be encouraged: a degree is an achievement, but it's not difficult to get. If you can last for three years at a university and still remember the name of your course at the end, you will get a degree.

Courses

You will be surprised how much less there is to your course than you thought from the prospectus. It will turn out to be less than the sum of its parts, especially if you're doing maths. For instance, you wouldn't expect someone studying French and German to be able to converse in the language. They're studying the literature – most probably in the English translation.

A mathematician might go for three years and never see a number except for zero, one and infinity. English students will unthinkingly rely on their PC's spelling software to cheque every peace they right. Hence, every year there are thousands of English graduates who can't write a job application letter, linguists who can't speak, mathematicians who can't add up, business graduates who borrow money off you, historians who can't remember where they were last night, and psychologists who rub everyone up the wrong way because they have absolutely no idea how people tick, and so go on to lucrative careers in personnel management.

If you feel you 'shouldn't be there' or are 'doing the wrong course', don't worry. Everyone thinks that (particularly your tutors). Most students are doing their course because:

- their school told them to do it
- their brother/sister/friend/father did it
- it was the only course with places left.

Fortunately courses are specifically tailored to the needs of the average bluffer. If you want to get a rough preliminary overview of your subject (enough, say, to pass final exams), the introduction in the course book will tell you all you need to know.

If, as you approach finals, you are worried that you cannot remember anything you have studied over the previous three years and are merely 'cramming', consider this:

1. Ninety-five per cent of work done by the average student is done in the three weeks before finals. (The other five per cent *is* finals.)

2. Cramming is a valuable life skill in itself, as anyone preparing a business presentation can tell you.

3. Most of the students who pass, if re-tested a year later, remember next to nothing of what they were supposed to have been studying.

4. Little of use is actually learned at university (if you don't count the things you're not supposed to learn).

5. Final exams are still designed to test what you do know, not what you don't. Your knowledge can be one-dimensional, lopsided, incomplete, superficial, or simply wrong, and you'll still pass.

Interviews

Under no circumstances should you try to talk about your subject at university interviews unless you have no option. You will have little chance of bluffing your way past university dons; they have had a decade or two more experience than yourself at the game.

Instead, talk enthusiastically about extra-curricular activities, the more outlandish the better. It contributes to the image of the well-rounded individual, ideally so spherical that you can be easily pushed around. For example, you might talk about:

a) your summer spent canoeing in the Spitzbergen islands
b) your trip across the Himalayas by bicycle
c) your year off fighting as a mercenary in Colombia (which leaves it open as to which side you were fighting for – government or drug barons).

Interviewers like this: it relieves the tedium of interviewing, and gives them a chance to show off their knowledge of South American politics, or (for younger tutors) their familiarity with the drug culture.

STARTING OUT

Essential Items

You need not pay too much attention to the list of suggested items to take that the university student union sends you. Typically it will advise you to bring things like 'coffee mugs, teapot, smart clothes, linen bag, plenty of paper and pens, several passport photographs of yourself, an alarm clock...' Instead make sure you have as many of the following items as you can take:

a) light bulbs
b) posters and plenty of adhesive
c) corkscrews, one of which must not work
d) large ashtrays
e) beer mugs and wine glasses
f) synthesiser, saxophone/drums/guitar with 250W amplifier.

If you don't smoke, drink or play an instrument you will have plenty of chances to do so. In any case you are supposed to be broadening your horizons, mixing with people with a wide range of interests, and catching things off them.

You certainly don't need an alarm clock. You know when it's time to get up by the smell of lunch wafting up from the campus café. Having a spare light bulb when the one in the loo gives out will do wonders for your popularity. The posters will be necessary to cover up the unsightly marks left on the wall by previous occupants of your room who have thoughtlessly hung posters everywhere. The corkscrews will be your most useful possession: those who don't have one will have to invite you to their parties to open the wine. If people call round to borrow your corkscrew without inviting you to the party, lend them the one that doesn't work.

Rather than take ordinary supermarket tea bags, take tins of 'proper' tea – Oolong, Lapsang Souchong, Assam, Earl Grey, English Breakfast, Orange Marmalade, and so on. By passing yourself off as a tea connoisseur you not only cultivate a sophisticated image, but justify the tea leaves in the bottom of the mugs and the brown rim stains by looking surprised and saying "but real tea is supposed to be like that". If anyone finds the taste unpleasant (yourself, for instance) blame the water: it's too acidic, too alkaline, or too neutral. Alternatively, take the Marxist view that proper tea is theft.

If you must take a teddy bear never try to keep it hidden; you'll only look a prat when you're found out. Better to keep it prominently displayed, possibly take it to lectures with you. Think of Sebastian in *Brideshead Revisited*: you'll still look a prat, but a confident and self-assured prat.

Finally, take something conspicuous and totally useless, such as a six-foot Chinese screen or a harmonium or a hatstand, to give your room that air of 'individuality'.

Arrival

There are a number of tedious things to be done in the first or 'Freshers' Week'. (First-years are called 'freshers' for a term by everyone else as a mark of deep contempt because they had to suffer it themselves in their first year.) You have to open bank accounts, trudge round to see tutors, buy books, get registered with the doctor, make friends, etc. One thing you certainly don't have to do is get down to work yet, for Freshers' Week is traditionally a time when nothing at all happens; you will have an opportunity to work after the hectic settling-in period, say in the middle of your third year.

The most important things to know about your area are the locations of:

1. The cheapest restaurants
2. Pubs to which students don't go
3. Asian grocery stores which are open at eight-thirty in the evening, seven in the morning* and Sunday
4. Twenty-four hour condom machines.

When you arrive you will be directed to your room by the porter of your Hall. University porters are all called Jim, and good relations are worth cultivating. This can be achieved by simply nodding as you go past him every morning and evening and saying "All right, Jim?", and giving Jim a bottle of sherry at Christmas. Porters are extremely powerful people, more so than tutors, and almost as much as the senior kitchen staff. Having the porter on your side will be invaluable when:

a) you have very noisy parties in your room
b) you want to put up those twelve backpackers you picked up in Italy in your Hall, and
c) you have locked yourself (and companion) out of your room at two in the morning

...in other words, most nights of the week. In case all three situations occur simultaneously, it's as well to

* Most first-years are awake at seven – 10 per cent have woken up to study, 90 per cent haven't gone to bed yet.

have a spare bottle of sherry to hand.

There are three types of beds, to go with the three types of neighbours you may have:

1. Attractive, but noisy and unstable.
2. Stiff and formal, look older than they are.
3. Comfortable at first, but soon turn out to be mysteriously irritating.

This uninviting furniture is supplied in the naïve belief that students lead a one-student, one-bed existence (or the equally naïve belief that it will deter them from doing otherwise).

Reconnaissance

Ascertain the whereabouts of all the key points in the building, viz. the lavatory, the bathroom, the fridge, and the telephone. The maximum number of bathrooms, toilets and telephones per thousand students is stipulated in the Building Regulations in order to provide mathematicians with data for Queueing Theory, especially on Sunday mornings.

There are great advantages to be had for the bluffer who arrives a day or two early. Remove the signs from the nearest lavatory and bathroom and replace them with 'Private' or 'Fire Exit'; that way you'll be guaranteed sole use of the said amenities for the first few days. Telephones are more difficult to disguise so an 'Out of Order' sign may have to do. Also, find out where the fire escapes are, not just in case of conflagration but for when the porter finds out who changed the signs. If the fire escape turns out to be a toilet, you'll know you're in good company.

Fridges are very useful but you should know how to use them. Don't just put your name on your stuff. Anything labelled 'Mike's milk, do not touch' gets emptied immediately. Instead, affix to your carton a large orange label bearing the legend: 'HAZARDOUS CHEMICAL' and write in red felt pen *'Radiated 13 March – Sample no. 05674/ MN/x-26'.*

Or invest in food colouring to turn your milk green and your butter blue. That'll deter thieves.

Friends

Circles of friends in week one tend to contain about ten to twenty people. The first few days are spent blissfully asking everyone their A-level results and going in large groups to restaurants. Remember never to organise the collection of contributions and payment of the bill which always, for as yet not fully understood reasons, comes to more than everyone's correct share put together. The second night you all go out, insist on a split-the-bill-evenly-between-us arrangement, and order the most expensive dish on the menu. Similar rules apply in pubs.

Don't fall into the trap of giving a build up to your pre-university friends/boyfriends/girlfriends if they come to visit. "You must meet Steve, he's amazing," a student will say, "a real lunatic." You can guarantee that when Steve comes for the weekend, he makes even the nervous intellectuals look exciting.

Never admit to still having friends from school. If you must mention them do so in a way that implies you've grown out of them – independence impresses. If they visit you, claim you met them while climbing Kilimanjaro or working in a factory during a holiday job.

Know Your Student

Bluffers are never overawed by the other students wandering round the campus and the Halls; they know that far from there being thousands of students in the university as it might seem, there are in fact only six:

1. **Rugby Players**. They have names like John and Gary and Stuart. They drink far too much, think everyone else is weak and ineffectual, shout at people, and only work when they have to. Twenty years later they have all turned into company executives and managers and get paid for doing all this.

2. **Awesome Intellectuals**. Typical names are William, Derek, Colin, Anne and Mary. They wear anoraks and glasses, work all the time and are only ever seen scuttling between their room and the library. They spend their three years convinced that they are not working hard enough and will fail their finals, and end up getting huge firsts.

3. **Public School Products**. They have names like Jolyon, Adam, Jacintha and Charlotte. Half of them condemn public schools and the Conservative Party and the other half condemn comprehensives and the Labour Party, but they all mix exclusively with other public school types and all mysteriously get very good jobs in their uncle's company on graduating.

4. **Christians**. Universally known as 'God squad'. Called Matthew or Louise. They never drink or smoke too much, nor get into trouble for having loud parties. On graduating, they go to Rwanda for

two years' voluntary work. To everyone's utter amazement, they actually seem to enjoy student life.

5. **Hacks**. Keep changing their name according to who they are trying to impress. Over-ambitious, self-centred and nauseating students who backstab their way to positions of responsibility in the Union/ Student Newspaper and ultimately the BBC/any political party/Parliament.

6. **Trendies**. Usually have assumed names, deliberately misspelt. Profess to like music but shout above it in clubs. Talk about ecstasy but can't spell it. Their clothes will be out of fashion next year but revived 20 years hence.

Don't make the mistake of thinking that other students are dreadfully clever, frighteningly high-class and awfully witty and urbane. Assume that everyone else is not too bright, working to middle class and thinks 'urbane' is a district council.

Know Your Tutor

'Tutor' is the safest term to describe anyone who teaches you at university. There are a variety of official posts whose names are misleading: professors don't profess to teach anything, for example, because they have become so good at their subject they can leave all the tedious business of giving desperately dull first-year lectures to those lower down the academic scale. These are given not by lecturers, but by recent graduates in order to finance their research.

Tutors come in three distinct types:

The Whiz Kid Graduate

The whiz kid graduate type is thirtyish but looks 17. They will give you four-hour tutorials at eight in the morning. They mark your essays assiduously, find all the mistakes, make you feel as if you know nothing and never miss a tutorial. They know everything about their own narrow subject.

The Middle-aged Tutor

The middle-aged tutor is fortyish but dresses like a trendy teenager – of 1980. They wear faded shirts, leather jackets and jeans. They say they look forward to getting to know you better when they first meet you and spend the next three years being mysteriously unavailable. These tutors keep your essay for weeks and only when you remind them does it reappear, with ticks at random intervals down the side and *'some interesting points'* at the bottom.

They talk about interesting but totally irrelevant things in tutorials and make you feel as if what you know isn't half as interesting as you thought it was. They know something about everything.

The Old Tutor

The old tutor is 70 but looks 110. The remarkable longevity of some academics may be explained by the fact that their demise can go unnoticed by their colleagues and students for several years.

Old tutors forget your name, but not the mistakes in your essays. They don't talk much in tutorials, preferring to let you ramble on until you make a fool of yourself. They know everything about everything.

Whenever you want to criticise your tutors, you can point out that in real life administrators become administrators because they are good at administering, teachers become teachers because they are good at teaching, and so on. At university, it is different: administrators become administrators because they are good at teaching (or more usually, because they are bad at teaching) and teachers become teachers because they are good at doing research. Remember you will only have to put up with tutors for a year or so each; if they had gone into real life, they could have been your employers.

Conversations

You will spend a lot of time talking to other students. Fortunately there are only five student conversations, so you can decide what to say well in advance. Not only does this make you seem more confident and clear-thinking, it saves you hours of wasted time later, repeating your lines of argument to convince yourself you're right.

1. What you did the year before

For the duration of the first week, you will be asked endlessly what A-levels you did, closely followed by whether you took a year out between school and university.

As no-one will actually remember what you tell them you can just make up anything which sounds interesting at the time. If you forget other people's details (and there's no particular reason to remember them) you can assume everyone comes from either

London or Manchester and did English A-level.

There is occasional controversy about whether or not taking a year off is a Good Thing; it always is. In fact, two years off is better, ten or twelve better still. Those who have taken time off before going to university are generally more mature as people, though the first few weeks of student life will soon change that. Claim, therefore, to have taken a year or two off even if you haven't. If you look 17 or 18, say you took A-levels a year or two early.

Your 'year off' should have been spent 'gaining experience', a meaningless phrase which sounds important. The same rules apply as in the interview. Good for 'experience' would be a year off having walked the Americas from Alaska to Tierra del Fuego, done Voluntary Service Overseas teaching English to mercenaries in East Timor, or something equally adventurous and wholesome. Claiming to speak some abstruse language that you've picked up in your travels gets points, and has the advantage that no-one can challenge you on your knowledge of Sioux Indian or Kamchatka dialect.

2. Sex

Strictly, *sexuality*. Sex is doing it, whereas sexuality is talking about it. Men should generally take the liberal, open-minded line that "None of us is one hundred per cent straight", but not within range of any rugby players.

It's regarded as a sign of emotional maturity to be able to talk about one's inner feelings in the intimate atmosphere of a late-night coffee with close friends. If you are completely heterosexual, have never worn clothes of the opposite sex, find no gratification in being walked over by men or women in high heels and have no interesting fetishes or emotional reactions unusual for your gender, invent some.

3. Politics

The anti-establishment, left-wing student who persists in challenging 'the system' brings general disapproval. You can justify being as anti-establishment as you like by asking why 'the system' should set up universities specifically to train inquisitive young minds to question and criticise existing ideas, and then complain when students do just that.

Use this to defend any outlandish view – that one day the country will have true anarchy/money-and-possession-free societies/proportional representation, and so on. Do not decry these beliefs though; argue about them by all means, but only on grounds of principle, never of practicality. Universities have never been concerned with the practicalities of anything, and there is no reason to create a precedent.

Feminism always crops up sooner or later. As usual, you can argue values of the present or distant past either way, but your parents are always wrong.

a) Our grandparents' generation got it right/wrong because men were in charge and everyone knew their place, namely in the mine/kitchen. Children learned that men ruled. They learned this from the head of the house – the mother.

b) Our parents' generation got it wrong because they said men and women were the same but they'd just been brought up to be different by their grandparents, who were to blame.

21

c) Our generation has got it right/wrong because we believe men and women are fundamentally different. Their 'brains are wired in different ways', as our grandparents always said. ("Research proves that women can't read maps/men are colour-blind", etc. Or vice-versa. Make up anything plausible.)

Racism is another old favourite. A good subject to discuss is the difference between the reception afforded to white students speaking at a union meeting, and to black students: the former get catcalled, whistled at, shouted down, heckled, beer thrown at them, etc., while the latter get a respectful hush and undivided attention. You should have strong views one way or the other about this positive discrimination, though it doesn't really matter which way, so long as you are fervently anti-racist.

Believe in what you say passionately, but remember there is a difference between beliefs (things you think are true but can't prove) and dogma (things you don't necessarily think are true and can't prove, but say anyway just to annoy people). Beliefs are in, dogma is out; besides it's smelly and difficult to wipe off your shoes if you tread in it.

4. Vegetarianism and wholefood

Claim to be some sort of vegetarian, even if it's the type that eats fish and meat. Diet is a favourite topic and you must acknowledge the following points:

a) vegetarianism is very healthy
b) people think vegetarian food is all the same, but there are *hundreds* of different dishes
c) vegetarianism doesn't exploit animals.

You can then go and have your Big Mac in peace.

Even meat eaters must be resolutely pro-wholefood and anti-additive. All E numbers are poisonous and carcinogenic. Invent some spurious ailment – runny nose, blotchy skin, lack of sleep – and tell earnestly of how, when you cut out tinned pilchards, it stopped. Allergies to additives are very popular and you must claim to have one or two, to E... (any number between four and five hundred). This was the one in the tinned pilchards.

5. That weird student down the corridor

Every corridor has at least one strange person who provides a permanent topic of conversation. Have a credible reason which explains the strange behaviour ("His father's in jail, of course", perhaps, or "Her mother's a professor of mathematics at Oxford"). As the subject won't be present, no-one will be able to argue with you.

Reputation

The first week or two establishes your reputation for the next three years, so you must choose what you do and say with care. In particular, be careful to avoid:

a) making no friends from your own year, or
b) making too many friends from your own year.

Similarly be very wary of:

a) sleeping with too many people too quickly
b) not sleeping with anyone before very long.

If you do any of these you will get 'a reputation', not for anything in particular, just 'a reputation'. This is the worst thing that can happen to anyone. Do not get a reputation.

Image

Now that over half of school leavers go on to higher education, the line between student and non-student fashion has virtually disappeared. Gone are the stereotype 'students' of bank leaflets and magazine ads in John Lennon glasses and a scarf made of deck chair material. Now they are portrayed more like clean-cut, smiling children's TV presenters.

Like everyone else, students spend a great deal of time and money on their image. The usual rules apply when trying to decide if something is fashionable or not: it must be uncomfortable, and it must be too skimpy to keep you warm.

Being recognisable as a student might have some advantages in some areas of town – you can practise your self-defence for example – but generally the whole idea of being a student is to dress so that you don't look like a student. It's the perfect excuse to re-invent yourself. You can suddenly get enough facial piercings to set off the alarm in the faculty library. You can dye your hair tangerine, or shave it off. You can change your name, rewrite your past, construct a whole new image and impress everyone. Until of course, your parents visit and blow your story utterly, handing round embarrassing school photos to your friends and addressing you by your real name.

You can usually tell what subject students are studying by the clothes they wear. Some are obvious:

bright trendy clothes are a sure sign of a modern linguist; anoraks and steel-rimmed glasses denote a chemist or engineer. The clothes should reflect your subject: literature devotees favour the intensely personal and bizarre; psychology students will prefer the lightweight and casual; philosophers go for anything old, heavy, and dark; scientists will only be interested in safe and established concepts which have been around for years.

In every corridor in every Hall of Residence there's the male student who dresses 'smartly' in a jacket, collar and tie, pullover, trousers and sensible shoes. These people always become dons or accountants and eventually go bald but persist in combing their hair over the bald patch so that the parting gets lower and lower. They spend their last years complaining about the ridiculous hairstyles and clothes worn by young people.

Exceptions to the above are graduates, of course. Graduates all dress identically in jeans, national health glasses and cycle clips, and carry little rucksacks with them everywhere. The only way to tell how many years they have been a graduate is to divide the length of their beard by three.

Haircuts are naturally central to your image. If you don't want to go to a run-of-the-mill hair salon with a pun on the word 'cut' in its name, your first option is to go down the road to the run-down old barber's. For the price of a drink you can ask for any style, but whatever you want you always get a short back and sides. Your second option is to go to a really exclusive place where a group of highly-trained hair designers will gather around you, give you coffee and explain their plans for your new image. For the price of a very large round you get a wealth of talent and skill working on you, but whatever you want you always get a short back and sides.

Depending on the circles you actually move in and would like to move in, you can go to one and say you went to the other.

Living In v Living Out

Whether to live in university accommodation or to live in a house, perhaps sharing with other students, is one of the great debates of university life. In fact they're as bad as each other, but vigorously justify whichever option you have chosen or have had to accept.

Living In

Living in is characterised by the Hall of Residence – a large building with a rabbit warren of corridors and thousands of pigeonhole-like rooms in which pets are not allowed (in order that you can't find out if they are wide enough to swing a cat).

Disadvantage: Hall rooms are generally cramped, stuffy and uncomfortable. They are deliberately designed like this in the fond hope that it will encourage students to go to the library.

Advantage: It is possible to wake up, put a record on, make a cup of coffee, toast six slices of bread, and reach over to the desk to play Tomb Raider 3, all without ever getting out of bed.

Disadvantage: There is no rationale behind the location of university accommodation: you could be quite near your lectures and your tutors, or you could be quite far away from them.

Advantage: You could be a very long way away indeed.

Advantage: With any luck there should be some useful amenities close by, such as gymnasia and squash courts. The great plus of these is not the capability for exercise but the often-overlooked showers which are always empty on Saturday nights or Sunday mornings, when everyone else will be queueing nine deep in Hall.

Living Out

Living out usually means sharing a house. Sooner or later every student has to come to terms with it. If the university cannot help you and your friends (as they will be for the first couple of weeks in the house) to find a place, you may have to scour various notice boards round the union or go to an agency.

Advantage: Living in a shared house is a splendid experience because it teaches you comradeship, the dynamics of how social groups interact in real life, and how to get on with people.

Disadvantage: This is accurately summed up by: 'If someone pinches your milk, you pinch someone else's.'

Disadvantage: Shared houses can be shabby, badly equipped and lack privacy.

Advantage: This is a perfect excuse for:

a) not bothering to clean or tidy up
b) spending the evening with that friend or potential
   partner in Hall.

Disadvantage: Your landlord may be a merciless exploiting capitalist.

Advantage: This is a politically rich situation to complain about.

Food

Your options are to eat in the university dining hall or cafés on campus, to eat out, or to cook your own meals. Eating in is cheap but can be dull – not because of the food, which is usually quite good, but the company, which will consist of people complaining that they could make better stuff than this themselves for half the price. Eating out is pricier but can be exciting, not because of the food which is usually no better than you would get on campus, but the thrill of the unexpected, such as extras on the bill.

Cooking your own is the best option. Being able to cater for yourself, or rather, appearing to do so, is part of the whole art of bluff. Of course, most of the time you will eat takeaways or make toast on your electric fire, but occasionally you should invite a few friends round for a meal. Student cuisine consists solely of:

a) spaghetti bolognese
b) cauliflower cheese
c) 'curry'.

Just being able to prepare one of these will be plenty, while being able to do all three (or claiming to do so) makes you sound capable and self-sufficient. The advantage of the last option when friends come to dinner is that in India there is no such thing as a standard curry, so you can make it with any ingredients you like, with any combination of spices, as hot or mild as you please and claim your style is the authentic one ("in the style of Rajasthan" – that sort of thing). If you are congenitally unable to cook anything at all, become a vegan. This saves you from bothering and means you can avoid expensive restaurants on the grounds that there is nothing on the menu you can eat. The only dish you need to be able to make then is 'salad'.

Money

Take any viewpoint on this. (The student loan system is vital/terrible and will boost/cripple the economy now that tertiary education is available to everyone/no-one, and so on.)

The only certain thing about money is that you will barely have enough – unlike your situation after you leave university, lose your student discounts, and start work, when you will never have enough.

When it comes to opening your bank account, whatever you do, don't go to your local branch. The further away from your bank manager (i.e. interviews on how you're going to work off your debts), the better. Open your account at the most distant bank from where you live, e.g. if at Exeter, open an account at the Kirkwall, Orkney, branch of the Bank of Scotland.

You can always justify spending money by insisting that economy of any kind is a false economy. This usually goes down pretty well with parents and relatives back home and will often elicit 'loans'. For instance, it is sound financial sense to buy expensive clothes and candlelit dinners for two since cheap clothes need replacing more often and cheap food could be riddled with Salmonella.

Relationships

Students are probably no more wanton than anyone else but the high-speed and concentrated nature of university life means that opportunities come thicker and faster.

For straight men

There are two types of women:

a) women with boyfriends at university
b) women with boyfriends back home.

Alternative classifications exist, viz: good looking/non-good looking women, slim women/fat women, brilliant women/dim-witted women, etc., though in practice there is a remarkable correlation between each respective category. The age-old problem applies: all the desirable women go out with Judo instructors, body builders, or obscure older men back home.

For straight women

There are three types of men:

a) nice men (a.k.a. other people's boyfriends)
b) creepy men (a.k.a. the ones who want to be your boyfriend)
c) bastards (a.k.a. the one who is your boyfriend).

You can be sure that when a woman says "Dave's really nice", she means "I don't fancy Dave at all". Women who fall for a man who is 'nice' either find out that he's gay or, more commonly, that he's only being nice because he thinks she's ugly and feels sorry for her. Creepy men are everywhere but are usually the first ones to announce that they're getting married or engaged, usually to someone nobody's ever heard of. Bastards make up the remaining 99 per cent.

For gays

There are two types of gays:

a) quiet gays
b) gays who wouldn't know what personality to have, what friends to make or what to talk about at all if they weren't gay.

If you've been in the closet for years, university is not a bad place to come out: being gay means you have a strong sexuality which is of course very fashionable.

Going out with someone at university is not as straightforward as it might seem. First, gossip travels amazingly fast in student communities, and anything you've done the night before will be common knowledge by the next morning. Second, in real life 'going out' with someone means staying in bed most of the time and not really going out anywhere. At university, you can go out with lots of people – to discos, pubs, concerts, meetings, lectures – and it's often difficult to tell if you're actually going *out* with them, or just going out with them. The only way of finding out who you're going out with may be to ask around.

ORGANISING YOUR TIME

To get the best out of your years at university you need to combine work with leisure in the most effective proportion.

Remember that future employers aren't really interested in how many discos you visited, or what you talked about over coffee to your friends, or what degree you have, they want to know what clubs you were a member of and what 'positions of responsibility' you held. They think that by knowing what position you played in the Engineering Faculty Soccer Third Team or that you were President of the Anglo-Inuit Society they can tell just how good an accountant you are going to be. It is therefore imperative that you join a few societies, play a few sports and 'do something' in the student union.

Clubs and Societies

In a typical university there will be something like one club or society for every ten students, which gives you an idea of the average membership of each. At the beginning of the first term there will be some sort of 'freshers' fair' where the clubs and societies are present. Each one has members handing out leaflets, and stalls where you can ask an embarrassing question like how many members they actually have. The main clearing banks are there too, hoping to drum up business. Students flock round them, not to find out about overdraft facilities, but to take armfuls of their free carrier bags.

Don't make the mistake of signing up for dozens of societies whose meetings you will never ever go to.

Pick one unlikely club (most university clubs are unlikely, but generally the more oriental, the better) and join that. You may well never go to a meeting in the next three years, but nobody will know that. The mere fact of being a member of the Japanese *Go* Society renders you an apparent instant expert on things oriental and gets you several thousand points. Prepare a superficially profound explanation of what *Go* (or whatever your club activity) is: "The rules are simple, yet it's a far deeper game than chess"; "It involves eastern philosophy..." You can adapt this to any other club activity.

The most important thing is *to get into a position of responsibility as soon as possible*. This is never difficult: just decide between yourself and the other member who is to be President and who is to be Secretary, and future employers will never fail to be impressed.

Drama

Drama is a very good field for bluffing, because no-one really knows what is good and what is bad. Being 'involved in a production' is excellent for your image, especially if it's something fashionable and fringe – along the lines of Women's Theatre stagings of unknown African mime dramas. As there will be no-one in the audience, afterwards you can claim anything you like about how it went.

Sport

Being good at genuine sports is excellent for your image but difficult to bluff, so uncoordinated types should take up some curious minority sport such as aikido or tiddlywinks and represent the university at that. This is usually a simple matter of telephoning the nearest university and deciding when the next match is to take place.

Pub types wanting to do some sport can always play for one of the numerous darts teams and challenge their neighbouring Halls of Residence at going round the board in doubles (darts optional).

Student Bands

Playing in a band is virtually essential for any self-respecting student. The only important things to tell people about are not the name of the band or what instrument you play but:

a) which bands have "influenced" you
b) how you "could have signed" for record company X but said no, and
c) your artistic differences with the other members.

Whether you play in a group or not, you can still go and listen to student bands. Whatever opinion you have about them should be political, forceful, exactly the opposite of what everyone else thinks, and reveal nothing about the music.

Union Politics

Getting involved in student politics is very easy. It requires no commitment, and it doesn't matter what your real beliefs are. So long as you stand for election to any student union post on the 'I'm not political' ticket you'll be voted in easily, and any union post is seen by employers as a 'position of responsibility'.

Even if you are not on the committee, you should go to union meetings. Motions at these meetings do one of three things:

1. Demand that this union writes letters to third world dictators requiring them to release political prisoners celebrated in songs by bands you've never heard of.

2. Demand that your university honours/refuses to honour some meaningless television celebrity, such as a former Prime Minister.

3. Demand that the university puts a long-life light bulb in your Hall lavatory.

In practice, there is more chance of (a) happening purely in deference to your letter, than there is of (c).

Relaxation

Knowing how to relax is the most important skill at university, and you must acquire it before you start on your course work.

Entertainments

Always call these 'ents'. Student ents cover a wide range from the terribly profound to the profoundly terrible; the usual sort of thing is a disco and/or a student band.

Never go to a disco before 11.45; when you do arrive, say you've been to a Polish film or a lecture on Biological Diversity.

Always declare that the disco or band was useless, but that you had a great time anyway. The amount sweated, multiplied by the size of the group of friends you went with, is taken to be indicative of how much you enjoyed yourself.

Parties

There are two types of student party.

1. Hall of Residence Room Parties

Usually spontaneous. Vary enormously in quality, but typically a few people "for coffee" that goes on till dawn. Can be fun, but the best reason for these is to make sure that the room's occupants can't finish their essays which are due in tomorrow. Then the fact that you haven't finished yours either doesn't look so bad.

2. Shared House Parties

The rules here are that:

a) All invitations state the starting time as '8'. Don't be fooled, this means 'when the pubs close'.

b) You should interpret 'PBAB' as 'please bring a bottle of the cheapest red from the corner shop'.

c) If you want to keep a drink to yourself, conceal it in a bottle marked 'Cherry Brandy'. This is sure to be left untouched until absolutely everything else has gone.

Drinking

The trick is to give the appearance of having drunk lots and lots without actually having done so. This is easier than it sounds. Keep surreptitiously filling your paper cup with water and draining it extravagantly in one. The advantage of people thinking you are drunk when you are not is that you will be forgiven for doing anything you wish because you were not responsible for your actions.

If you do find yourself drinking more than you anticipated, the stages of drunkenness are:

1) Sober. People understand most of what you are saying, but don't really listen.

2) Tipsy. People listen to you hoping you will say something embarrassing.

3) Drunk. People don't understand what you are saying and stop listening.

4) Very drunk. *You* don't understand what you are saying.

5) Horribly drunk. You have perfectly intelligible conversations, but only with other people who are horribly drunk. Horribly drunk people often have no recollection of what they did after they got very drunk; it's nature's way of preserving self respect.

Do not attempt to drive a car or motorbike in any stage past (1).

Do not attempt to write an essay in stage (4) or (5) unless absolutely critical.

Do not attempt to listen to a student band in stages (1) to (3).

OTHER ACTIVITIES

There are many other things you can do with your spare time, some of which you can profitably spend on your course work, though it shouldn't interfere too much. Have no qualms about working as economically as possible because:

a) the last thing most tutors want is a student who knows more about the subject than they do

b) the essays they like marking least are the longest and most detailed ones

c) so long as you don't fail your degree, your actual or expected grade makes no difference at all to prospective employers.

The approach you should take to work is that which you would use for paying tax. Supply too much once, and they'll expect that amount all the time; keep to a reasonable level and you have leeway in both directions. Avoid it legitimately wherever possible, but keep all your paperwork up to date, and use all the time available for giving it in.

Remember that universities do not exist to let students study. Teaching students is a technical requirement to give the establishment some sort of credibility.

Reading Lists

As soon as you arrive you will have the reading list thrust into your hand. Do not attempt to read it all, that would be too much hard work (the list, that is, not the books themselves – the fact that students never read the books is taken as read, as it were). The reason there are so many books listed is to show how clever your tutors are and how many books there are whose titles they know.

You should read one of the books marked 'essential reading', then dig out the most arcane book you can discover on your subject in the university library, find an obscure parallel between the two, and announce this parallel to your tutor. This is a good tactic for two reasons:

a) it gives the appearance of having read thoroughly everything on the list and more; and

b) it enables your tutor (who is unlikely to have read the obscure book you mention) to bluff his or her way round the subject very convincingly. That is precisely how tutors get to be where they are.

You can thus pick up several tips on bluffing. Notice, for example, the classic response of tutors as you start talking about something they can't know anything about because you have just made it up. They start smiling as you get half way through, apparently listening attentively, then say "Ah, yes, but you see, one thing you've overlooked is..." and off they go on some completely unrelated topic.

Don't be impressed by the fact that most of the books on the list are written by your tutor. This is because:

1. They are sensibly ensuring their own livelihood by boosting orders at the university bookshop.

2. They have been frantically publishing papers about anything they can think of for the past two years

on the principle that when it comes to cuts in education, the first to go are those who haven't published a major paper or book in recent months.

Lectures

Never get into the habit of going to lectures just because you feel like it. It is quite easy to drift into the frame of mind where, instead of staying in bed working out how to make your first million, you decide to go to a lecture, thinking "If I don't go, I may miss something important". You are merely deluding yourself. The only things to know about lectures are that:

1. They are extremely dull.

2. It is impossible to maintain concentration for an hour, and therefore your notes will be incomprehensible when you look at them the next day. Far better to borrow and photocopy the impeccably neat, one-point type version from the brightest in your group.

If your own tutor is giving a series of lectures, things are different, of course; your absence must start from day one or else you might build some feeling of personal responsibility towards your tutor and feel you ought to go to every one.

If you must go to lectures, go to a couple in subjects you are not studying and remember something esoteric from each. This enables you to amaze other students with your all-round knowledge and has the benefit that you can choose lectures which coincide with the afternoons when you're not playing some sport, or the mornings when you're not in a rehearsal for your latest play. It also gives you plenty of material to talk about in tutorials to avoid your own subject.

Essays

Student work consists largely of essays – or, as tutors will call them, "your written work". The term is misleading since you won't have to put too much work in, and someone else will have written most of it. Perhaps that's why no-one talks about 'writing essays' but of 'doing' them.

The variants of your written work are assignments, projects, dissertations and so on. The longer they are, the more specific but less useful the conclusion. For example, a short essay might explain how an aeroplane can fly. A longer assignment or project might explain how an aeroplane can fly upside down. A dissertation, on the other hand, takes thousands of words and many months' work to decide that, if a bee were an aeroplane it wouldn't be able to fly.

Doing essays is rather like doing your washing; it's a boring fortnightly chore, taking ages if you try to produce a neat finished product with all the kinks ironed out, but just a couple of hours if you merely want to keep yourself covered. It is possible to download a 'model essay' on any subject from the Internet, and present it as your own work. Edinburgh University withheld the degrees of 90 students for alleged plagiarism, and Berkeley reported a sevenfold increase in cheating between 1993 and 1997. Some institutions are now scanning essays with software that looks for suspicious similarities of phrasing or vocabulary. But with more university courses being run on a production-line basis, and some class sizes up to 200, the chances of being caught out are slim. Even if your tutors happen to know the web sites that specialise in supplying essays, some free and some paid for, they can't stop you contacting another student, possibly on the other side of the world, and 'borrowing' their award-winning essay by e-mail.

It's a big problem for universities, and there's talk of degrees being worth less. Or even worthless.

But whether or not the cheats are found out it doesn't matter to you, because bluffing is not cheating. Cheating is making your tutor believe that someone else's hard work is your own. Bluffing is making your tutor believe that your own lazy work is pretty good.

To your tutor, talk scathingly about the web sites that offer 'model essays' for download ("dreadfully written... formulaic and lacking content... irrelevant to the particular assignment we've been set" will never be far wrong). This gives the impression of a well-researched, clear-thinking and honest student. Be careful about criticising specific sites though – one of them might be your tutor's. Or the one they themselves plagiarised for their PhD.

To your fellow students, maintain that you've seen all the essay web sites for this week's assignment, and only one is any good. Then you can either:

a) not tell anyone what it is, and retain some mystique (beginning of year)

b) make up a vague-sounding address, so that they all go looking for it, get sidetracked, and end up wasting their evenings surfing (middle of year)

c) give out the address of the worst site to people one by one in "strict confidence", and watch everyone else hand in identical dreadful essays (end of year, so that it's too late for them to get back at you).

It's a good idea to scan these web sites to get an idea of what's on offer, but you will write your essay in the time-honoured, traditional, rigorous and honest way – by rewriting the section from the Penguin Introduction the night before it's due.

Bibliographies

At the end of your essay, make an impressive-looking list of the books you didn't read. This is the Bibliography. Don't mention the books you did read, if any, because large chunks will appear thinly rewritten in your essay, and you shouldn't advertise the fact too much.

Using the Internet

Make full use of your free Internet access. Tell people about the fanzine web site you set up for some obscure band "as a hobby" – how it's now getting 5,000 hits a week, you are being besieged by companies wanting to advertise on your site, and your links to online CD shops are already producing commissions.

In reality, like everyone else, you will be busy e-mailing those Australian backpackers you met in Vietnam, wasting evenings on chat sites, insulting people on newsgroups, putting your holiday snaps on your home page, and downloading every piece of free software you can – but it's all good bluffing practice for when you apply for a job. The interviewers will be ten years older than you and intimidated by these millionaire student dot-com entrepreneurs they've heard about, and can't fail to be impressed.

Keeping your essays organised is vital. File your printouts into groups so you know which they are. The bad ones can be recycled as cigarette lighters, the good ones sold to the next year's students.

Tutorials and Seminars

The great thing at university level is that fundamentals are re-examined, so you can fearlessly ask obvious or even stupid-sounding questions as if you were hinting at some deep and far-reaching point about the foundations of the subject. Examples might be "How can we be sure one plus one equals two?" or "Was Latin the language of the Romans?" or "Who wrote *Twelfth Night*?" or "Is a vacuum empty?"

Keep asking these questions – tutors love talking, and if you choose the question so as to lead away from the subject of your essay, you don't need to have done the work to understand the subsequent discussion.

It's actually a good idea to go to a few tutorials and seminars if only so you can say you have been. Never push, shout at, abuse or strike a tutor, unless he/she attacks you first.

Avoiding Tutorials

In the limiting case of having been able to do no work at all, you may have to miss a tutorial. This is not recommended; tutors don't mind you coming to a tutorial when you haven't been able to do the work, because it gives them a chance to show how clever they are, but they get a bit upset if you don't show up, not because they're worried about your academic welfare but because consistently low attendances will be noticed and in the prevailing financial climate in academia, nobody's job is safe. In addition, if they had known you weren't going to turn up, they could have had the afternoon off.

If you must miss one, the following techniques or excuses have been found effective. It must be stressed that these are for emergencies only, when your absence is absolutely unavoidable – for example, if you have a family bereavement, or if there's a test match on television.

a) Giving Blood

Few tutors can criticise you for performing this valuable duty to society. It is best to choose a rare blood group to make your donations especially vital, say beta double minus. With luck, you can blame your subsequent inability to do any of the next week's work on lack of blood, and insist the shortfall in liquid be made good in the college bar.

b) Playing Sport for Your Country

Getting to international standard in most things can be tricky but is well worth the effort. Most universities have bizarre sports clubs with 'international' fixtures: frisbee throwing, underwater knur and spell, for example, and these are good places to start. Fixtures against the next Hall of Residence can be deemed 'international' if the teams retire to an Indian restaurant afterwards.

c) Attending Job Interviews

Say you went for a job interview by all means, but tailor your appearance accordingly. If, for example, you say you went to see an accountancy firm, 'return' wearing a suit; for an Internet startup company, wear T-shirt and baseball cap and come back having spent far more than you had planned, just like dot.com businesses.

Exams

In the run-up to any exams, there is always a desperate working through of past papers to see what questions came up in previous years. You know that this is a waste of time; exam questions are not chosen on the basis of what didn't come up last year or what hasn't been asked since 1983, they are selected at random at a meeting of examining tutors all impatient to get back to their research.

Don't bother with too many past papers, but claim an encyclopædic knowledge of which question came up when. Thus in the lunch queue, when someone says the Mongolian Transhumance Farming can't possibly come up, you smile and say "Well, it last came up in 1992, so it's due to come up again." If anyone mentions questions from last year's paper, frown as if searching your memory and say, "Mmm, yes, always comes up in successive years, that one... 1984 and 1985, 1994 and 1995... Could well be due again this year." The advantages of this are:

a) you worry all the other students into frantically revising the obscure parts of the syllabus;

b) you worry them even more because they can't work

out where you got the past paper for 1984 from;

c) you give the appearance of having done 25 past papers without needing to show any detailed knowledge of the answers.

An odd concept called 'exam technique' is often stressed in student guide books where you are given really useful tips like 'Write on one side of the paper at a time' and 'Make sure you read the question'.

For bluffers the following rules apply:

1. Write in very large (but illegible) handwriting to spin the length out, and as you stack up your finished pages at the side of the desk, slip in an extra two or three blank sheets for every page of your essay. That should make the other examinees panic as they watch your fifty-side opus growing; they have no way of knowing if it is only a garbled regurgitation of an essay you bought from someone the week before.

2. If you find the line of argument isn't flowing smoothly, disguise it by spreading the essay out over several out-of-sequence pages, so that the examiner has to work his or her way through page 1, followed by 2, then 6, then 3 including a paragraph omitted from page 7, then the lower half of 14 via 11, then page 5 renumbered as 9.

Vacations

Never 'holidays', which smacks too much of school. Don't think that vacations are for your benefit, to let you do your course work, for example. Their purpose is to let university tutors get on with their real work, their research, in peace. So you shouldn't undertake academic work during the vacation: you should be getting 'experience' in a holiday job working in a fish filleting factory in Hull or with depressed inner city families (who, after four weeks of student visits, are entitled to be depressed).

Vacations are a good time for visiting your friends from college – the further away they live the better. It scores several hundred points next term to mention casually that you went to see Michelle in Paris or Hamish in the Hebrides.

Travel

The point about vacation trips is not the going, but the telling everyone about your incredible experiences when you come back.

A common story which goes the round after the vacations is how, by an amazing coincidence, two students from the same Hall met in the same hostel in Bangkok. As 90 per cent of students go to the same places each summer, it would be far more amazing if they had both met in the faculty library. Make your story much more interesting. Your chance meeting was in an officially closed bar in a village not even on the map four days' ski from the nearest local railway line in the far north of Finland.

Student travel is kept artificially cheap. Despite the grumbles of ordinary people who have to pay full prices and effectively subsidise you, it is precisely for their benefit that student discounts on foreign travel are offered, to keep you out of the country.

Use the long break to go somewhere really exotic. Or rather, to talk about going somewhere really exotic, which is just as much fun. The more off the beaten track the place is, the better. Not Thailand, but Laos; not Nepal, but Uzbekistan; not Australia, but Papua New Guinea; not Egypt, but Namibia. Just having the Lonely Planet guides to such places on your bookshelf gives the air of someone rugged and well-travelled even if you are only "thinking of going there this summer".

When talking about places you have in fact visited, the usual rules for travel bluffing apply. The misread map which added an hour to your picnic site walk in Kathmandu becomes three days lost in the Himalayas. The clumsy landing aboard a South American jet becomes a near-crash caused by a hijacker, an earthquake and the pilot being locked in the toilet. You didn't take a camera because you're a traveller, and only tourists take snaps (hence your bluffs can't be called).

Dismiss the places anyone else has been – "You went to Shanghai? Yes, it used to be nice, but it's gone all touristy now. Xiao Xing's quite nice though..." Or "Yes, Quezaltenango's OK, but it's not the real Guatemala, is it?" and so on. You probably travel by the usual cheap and cheerful ways – coaches or Inter Rail tickets for Europe, Round the World plane tickets for South-East Asia, Australia and the US. But it sounds much more impressive to say you found some incredible last-minute (and therefore not disprovable) bargains "on the Internet". If you can convince people you found a flight to Budapest for the cost of a double-vodka and Red Bull, your status is assured.

Coming Back

Strange things happen to people during the summer vacations. A new first year arrives, first-years become second-years, second-years become third-years, third-years become graduates; the changes are not just arithmetical. You must know how to behave according to your own year, and how to treat the other years.

First-Years

Students in their first year are wide-eyed, enthusiastic about everything, go to restaurants in groups of twelve and stay up till four every morning drinking coffee in each others' rooms. They don't know any third-years but are impressed by second-years who are friendly to them. They either worship tutors, or are frightened of them.

Second-Years

After the novelty of the first year has worn off students become more cynical. They look down on first-years as immature. They look down especially on those second-years who are friendly with first-years, regarding it as unhealthy and vaguely pederastic. They concentrate on things that will look good on their job application forms:
- meaningless positions of 'responsibility' in eccentric societies,
- backstabbing student union posts,
- hack 'journalistic' activities in student papers that not even the students read,
- radio stations not even the students listen to,

and so on. They think all tutors know nothing.

Third-Years

As everything starts to repeat itself exactly for the third time round, third-years become extremely cynical. Linguists, who have spent a year abroad, are the most terminally cynical of all, and become awfully serious. As job-hunting season beckons third-years start to wander around wearing suits and clashing ties with expressions which say they'll soon be out of here, thank you. They hardly socialise with each other, never mind anybody else; they stay up till four every morning desperately doing all their first and second year work. They think some of their tutors are great people, while the rest know nothing.

Becoming a Graduate

There are two reasons why you would continue studying after taking your degree.

1. To continue to have a railcard and student discounts into your late 30s.

2. To get those magic letters 'Dr' before your name, so you can ask people who tell you all their health problems at parties to take all their clothes off. You don't have to tell them your doctorate was for your thesis on Roman Fireplace Construction in the Upper Danube and its Effect on Urbanisation Trends in Moesia, and not Medicine.

Though supposedly doing 'research', there is still plenty of room for bluffing. You can't be expected to discover anything significant in your postgraduate studies: the pace of research is so fast nowadays that you spend most of your graduate days plagiarising other people's work.

After three to seven more years of cheap travel, you complete your thesis and get your PhD (though abandoned PhDs are very common: there's a limit to the amount of time you can continue to be a member of the university, after which you can't get a student railcard). Your thesis gets filed away somewhere and nobody ever looks at it again, except future postgraduates looking for someone's work to plagiarise, so you can tell people it was about anything you like.

You can get a variety of letters after your name for all this – DPhil, PhD, MLitt, MA and so on, depending on the length and quality of your work, though as only postgraduates would appreciate the difference, any one set of letters is just as impressive as any other for all practical purposes, such as getting people to undress at parties.

Never be bluffed by an Oxford or Cambridge graduate: they get MAs automatically a few years after graduating, which is why they have to write 'MA (Oxon)' or 'MA (Cantab)'. It is not to show how clever they are at having studied there and knowing the Latin names as well; it is an admission that they got their MA not through two years of intense study but by sending off a cheque.

Bluffers who want to carry on bluffing their way even further through academia just like their tutors did can take heart from the following:

a) research gets so obscure at really high levels that no-one can tell the valuable from the worthless;

b) the cheap university accommodation, the number of in-house perks and lack of student bands enjoyed by the average tutor much more than makes up for losing that student railcard.

UNIVERSITIES

Britain

It's essential to know a little about universities other than your own. In Britain there are two types:

1. Campus
2. Others.

Campus types (Keele, Exeter, Nottingham, etc.) are more or less self-contained units where most students live, work and spend their leisure time. Student bars, sports facilities, Halls, student shops, libraries and lecture halls, etc., are all together on one large site, thus obviating the need for students ever to leave the university. This is a remarkably convenient and agreeable state of affairs – for the general public.

Others (Oxford, Cambridge, Manchester) are spread out around the cities, so that normal pub-goers, shop-keepers and other innocent members of the public are forced to mix with students every day. In fact, there isn't really a 'university' at either Oxford or Cambridge, only a collection of independent, more or less self-governing colleges. The reasons for this are partly historical and partly political (for example, to disguise the fact that between them the Oxbridge institutions own half of the land in the south of England by spreading it out amongst the colleges). The upshot is that:

a) students at these and other college universities (Durham, London, York) identify much more strongly with their college than the university.

b) American tourists who ask a student in the High Street in Oxford for the location of 'the university' only meet with hoots of laughter.

British universities also divide in the following ways:

1. Oxbridge

An all-encompassing term for Oxford (which came first) and Cambridge (which was set up a few years later by a bunch of Oxford rejects). Suffice to say that virtually all 20th-century British Prime Ministers came from Oxford – Margaret Thatcher did Chemistry there, and Harold Wilson got one of the highest Politics marks in Oxford's history. At any given time the Cabinet is full of Oxbridge graduates; clearly there is a lot to answer for.

Despite what you might think, a lot of people at the various Oxbridge colleges are actually quite clever, and every bit as responsible and mature as most other students, or even less so.

Oxford and Cambridge are made up of lots of effectively independent colleges. All you need know about them is that:

- New College, Oxford, is very old
- Caius College, Cambridge, is pronounced 'keys'
- the only people to have had colleges named after them at both universities are Jesus, St John, St Peter, Mary Magdalene* and Isaac Wolfson.

* Note: Magdalen College Oxford (pronounced Maudlin) is pronounced the same as, but spelt differently from, Magdalene College Cambridge, which is spelt the same as, and like Magdalen is also named after, but pronounced differently from, Mary Magdalene.

54

Everything else you have ever read or heard about Oxford and Cambridge is true, including most of the fiction. The Oxbridge institutions have been around so long you can hold whatever opinions you like about them and it won't make the slightest difference.

2. Quasi-Oxbridge
Edinburgh considers itself Oxbridge, and St. Andrews definitely is, if only because even the most mundane things there have Latin names, and it is the oldest university of them all.

3. London
London University is a federation of 40-odd colleges and institutes. These include University College, King's College and the London Business School, plus many intriguingly titled bodies such as the Institute of Romance Studies – not, sadly, anything to do with Mills & Boon.

4. City Universities
Examples are: Birmingham, Brunel (really Uxbridge), Manchester, Glasgow. There are lots of concrete buildings in the middle of the city to house the students which can sometimes be noisy, drab, dull and boring. (The buildings, that is.) There are strong local industrial links to the course content so it's great for anyone who thinks you go to university to study hard and get a good job in industry, because that is what usually happens. Good social atmosphere.

5. Country Universities
Examples: Exeter, Warwick, York. A lack of local

industrial links to the content of the course means that a high percentage of the inmates have a great time enjoying themselves in leisure activities and only working when absolutely necessary. Same for the students. Great social atmosphere.

6. Obscure Places Not On Standard Maps
Examples: Lampeter, Keele. Obviously no industry, and course contents which don't link up with anything. All miles away from the nearest town (and hence the nearest police stations, bank managers, etc). Fantastic social atmosphere.

7. Polytechnics-turned-universities
Examples: Brookes University (was Oxford Poly), John Moores University (was Liverpool Poly), De Montfort University (was Leicester Poly). All these silly names were chosen for the reason that it is impossible to tell which town the institutions are in any more, in a vain attempt to cut down on applications. Standards have risen markedly since the name changes, with the proportion of students gaining university degrees shooting up from 0% to 100%.

America

The concept of university in America is rather different from that elsewhere. All you need know about it is that they have two semesters instead of three terms, call it 'school' instead of university, collect credits towards a degree in any unrelated subjects, rather like sets of stamps, and take at least 15 years to collect enough of them to reach credibility. Most students finance themselves by doing 'work study' jobs on the university campus, which are not as they sound but more like a legitimised form of bonded slavery. Others borrow money from the government on very easy terms, so easy in fact that the government often neglects to collect the debts. There are also a wide range of scholarships available, some in exotic subjects such as American football, and even some in sports.

Deride the 'Seven Sisters', America's elite band of women-only colleges (Vassar, Wellesley, Smith, Mount Holyoke, Bryn Mawr, Barnard and Radcliffe), because the pressures of falling enrolments means that some are now letting male students through the doors rather than the dormitory windows.

Pooh-pooh all American universities as being of doubtful quality, even the top-notch 'Ivy League' ones (Brown, Cornell, Columbia, Dartmouth, Harvard, Pennsylvania, Princeton and Yale). Unless you get a chance to go to one, of course, in which case you leave for America immediately.

France

There is no application procedure in France like UCCA in the UK. If your average score for 'baccalauréat' (sort of Gallic A-levels) is high enough, you can just turn up without warning at your local university on the first day of term and enrol. The result is, predictably, complete chaos, with popular courses being drastically over-subscribed and only settling down when the drop-outs have left.

In common with other European systems, students study a variety of subjects and, because there are no grants, tend to go to their local university and live at home to save money. Such behaviour would be unthinkable for most British students; you wouldn't be able to drink, bring your lovers back or have riotous parties at home.

Germany

German students take their 'Abitur' – the equivalent of British A-levels – at 19, often followed by a couple of years' vocational training and a couple more of compulsory National Service. As a degree takes at least a further five years, German first-years can be as old as 24, and fresh graduates 30 or so. This means that, despite the liberal nature of German higher education, the students are extremely mature and conservative and produce very boring rag mags.

Japan

Competition to get into the best universities in Japan is fierce – many pupils go to cram schools every evening as well as doing their normal complement of work. They reckon if you sleep more than four hours a night you'll have no chance in the entrance exams. Graduates from the best universities (Tokyo being the tops) are automatically assured of the best jobs.

Once in, it's all a stream of lectures and essays learned by rote, and everyone passes in the end. As their time at university is the only opportunity the Japanese ever have to relax, they make the best of it by doing as little as possible. Japan, probably the hardest working industrialised nation in the world, has students that are just as idle as anywhere else.

GLOSSARY

All-nighter – Round the clock work (or other) session. Essays should always be done the night before the tutorial to ensure they are as up to date as possible.

BA – Standard degree. Stands for 'Bachelor of Arts', though a) married female students can also get them, and b) at Oxford all subjects, even nuclear physics, are classed as 'arts' and earn you a BA.

Bibliography – The most creative and imaginative part of an essay.

BSc – Science degree; Bachelor of Science. Should clearly therefore just be 'BS' but the extra 'c' is added to remind scientists how the word is spelt.

Careers advice service – Anything from a pile of glib leaflets and booklets which encourage a career as an accountant or banker, to detailed and lengthy computer-based personality questionnaires which find the best job for you, oddly enough usually accountancy or banking.

Curriculum Vitae (CV) – List of achievements to show prospective employers. Latin for 'pack of lies'.

DPhil/PhD – Doctor of Philosophy, earned by several years' post graduate study regardless of subject title, perhaps because at the end of ten years in higher education you have to be philosophical about the value of it all.

Freshers – Contemptuous term for newly-arrived first-years, until they go stale and hard like everyone else.

Graduate – In theory any person who has a degree, though usually applied by tutors to those doing further study, when it means a person who has only one degree.

Graduation ceremony – A scroll-on, scroll-off service.

Grant – Obsolete name for student unemployment benefit.

Going up/down – Students traditionally don't 'go to' or 'leave' but 'go up' to and 'come down' from Oxford and Cambridge, probably because for many of them it will be the furthest north they will go in their lives.

Honours degree – Clearly much more impressive than just a degree, though few people know or care what the difference is.

Matriculation ceremony – Being formally accepted into the university, from Latin *matrix*. Supposedly means 'womb', but more probably a reference to thousands of identical figures in rows and columns whose purpose is a complete mystery.

Milk Round – Series of visits to your university by big employers who show slides, ply you with plonk, feed you sandwiches, and then employ someone else. So called because they've given up hope of employing the cream.

MLitt – Like an MA but in Li*tt*erature.

MPhil – Similar to PhD but period of research, hence beard, is shorter.

MA/MSc – Master of Arts/Science. Title earned typically by one year's full-time, or two year's part-time study. Women get the same title, which is better than being called 'Mistress of the Arts'.

MBA – Master of Business Administration, one or more years' expensive and demanding full- or part-time study for prospective senior managers. A PhD gets you zero; and MBA gets you zero on the end of your salary.

NUS – National Union of Students, whose membership card is worth more than Diners Club, American Express and Visa put together, is less expensive, and doesn't get you on mailing lists.

Opting in – Only getting something if you sign up saying you want it. University accommodation, for example, is always 'opting in'. The list to sign is hidden on the 'Minor Sports' noticeboard behind last week's Pétanque third team.

Opting out – Having to pay for something unless you sign up saying you don't want it – breakfast, for example, is always opting out, because you have to get up that morning and go to the dining hall to sign the opting-out list, by which time you may as well have the breakfast.

PGCE – Post Graduate Certificate in Education: licence to teach in schools earned by a year's study. 'Those who can, do: those who can't, teach; those who can't teach, teach teachers.'

Postgraduate – Same as graduate. The 'post' is spurious, added to give the impression of a man (or woman) of letters.

Rag week – Week when students abandon their work to go on pub crawls and dress in ridiculous clothes, all for charity (as opposed to the rest of the time when they do these things anyway).

Rag mag – Magazine full of jokes, whose proceeds go to charity, made entirely of recycled material.

Red brick university – Recent universities built of grey concrete.

Resumé – American equivalent of CV, though less of a list and more of a mission statement. From French for 'wild exaggeration'.

Sandwich course – Main part of a quick meal for busy students, e.g. those doing a work experience year in the middle of their degree.

Seminar – Similar to a tutorial but with more people. Nothing to do with 'seminal' except that it is also a medium for blind reproduction.

Thesis – A postgraduate work which could earn you a doctorate, generally as long as the London telephone directory, and almost as exciting to read.

Tutorial – Similar to a seminar but with fewer people. Bright bluffers get through them by letting others do the talking, even in an individual tutorial.

Undergraduate – Term applied to someone studying for a degree, except when used by tutors when it means someone without even one degree.

Union bar – Cheap device designed to prevent you from going out and annoying the public.

THE AUTHOR

Rob Ainsley enrolled in the University of Life at the start of the 1960 academic year. He is currently heading for a third. He took a maths degree from Oxford in 1982 and never did give it back. His tutors had to admit they were surprised when he passed maths finals — most of them thought he'd been studying something else. The only one who remembers him said he would never do anything to further mathematics. In 1987 he wrote *Bluff Your Way in Maths*, so proving his old tutor right.

He started a teacher training course and made a significant contribution to secondary education by not becoming a teacher. For six years he edited the classical music magazine *Classic CD,* confirming the link between abilities in music and maths — he knows nothing about maths either.

From spring 1999 he travelled the world for 18 months, finishing his latest book — he's a slow reader. Never really sure where he lives or what he does, he has to keep looking at his web site (www. robainsley.com) to find out.

THE BLUFFER'S GUIDES®

The million-copy best-selling series that contains facts, jargon and inside information – all you need to know to hold your own among experts.

AVAILABLE TITLES:

Accountancy
Astrology & Fortune
  Telling
Archaeology
The Classics
Chess
Computers
Consultancy
Cricket
Doctoring
Economics
The Flight Deck
Football
Golf
The Internet
Jazz
Law
Management
Marketing
Men
Music

Opera
Personal Finance
Philosophy
Public Speaking
The Quantum
  Universe
The Rock Business
Rugby
Science
Secretaries
Seduction
Sex
Skiing
Small Business
Stocks & Shares
Tax
Teaching
University
Whisky
Wine
Women

www.bluffers.com